The Stuff
of Life

Home Made
Poems

by

Maddie
Williams

For Angie and
Maggie who both
encouraged me to
read my poems
aloud and to get
them into print.
Many thanks!

The Stuff of Life
Copyright Madeleine Williams 2018

All rights reserved.

Table of Contents

ANIMAL STUFF

Assorted Cats

Blue
eyes,
yellow
eyes, green
eyes,
Cat's eyes!

Long fur, short fur, sleek fur,
Cat's fur!

No tail, long tail, fluffy
tail,
Cat's tail!

Straight whiskers, curved whiskers,
twitchy whiskers,
Cat's whiskers!

Black cats, ginger cats,
tabby cats and torties,
Assorted cats!

Sleeping cat, hunting cat, playful cat,
Cat's life!

Cat Lover

I woke up this morning and I was
covered in cats!
I woke up in the night and I was
covered in cats!
One at my head and on my feet,
And one under the duvet enjoying the
heat.

I find that my kitchen is covered in
cats,
When I bring in the shopping its
covered in cats.
One on the window sill, two on the
hob,
And one in the bag seeking something
to rob!

I sit on my sofa and I am covered in
cats!
Watching TV I am covered in cats!
One kneading with her claws while
sitting on my lap,
One curled up close and having a nap.

Another stretched out having his
tummy fur smoothed,
And one at my feet hoping for food.

I go into the garden, its covered in
cats!
If I sit down I will be surrounded by
cats!
One by the pond and one on the fence,
One up a tree and one on the bench,
All enjoying the summer sun,
And watching for wildlife to have
some fun.

As I do my chores all eyes are on me,
They know I'm a cat lover, you see!

Cats and Dogs

I like dogs, but I *love* cats!
Dogs can be a faithful friend, but not
cats!
Dogs will follow you and do as you
bid.
Cats do as they please, I do not kid!

Dogs just sit and wait for their meal,
but not cats!
They will stare at you and circle you
and demand to be fed.
If you think you have trained them,
you are easily led.
Dogs will wait till its time for their
walk, but not cats.

Dogs always like you to play with a
ball,
Cats go off and don't need you at all.
Dogs stay by you and always at home.
But not cats!
Who knows how far they roam.

Give a dog a treat of chicken,
All they do is to gulp and some
licken.
But not cats!
Give them a treat and they take their
time,
They sniff, they lick and finally chew
and savour,
like we would a glass of wine.

Dogs will help you bring in the
shopping,
If they can see that you are struggling.
But not cats!
They will watch and glare with their
nose in the air,
As if to say, "I hope my food's in
there!"

You can put down the food for the
dog,
Who will gobble it down like a hog.
But not cats!

Their food will be treated with
caution, to check if is the correct
portion.
And if it is not they will turn their
back and go to next door for their
luncheon!

A dog will enjoy a holiday at the
seaside.
But not cats!
They don't like being caged, they
need to be outside.
So they stay at home and await your
return
And hope that you wont go away
again!

Fat Cat

Cleo was a fat cat and that was no
mistake,
But she really took the biscuit when
she ate the birthday cake!

Yes, she's very beautiful, but I
suggest you do not touch,
Especially if you value all your
fingers very much.

She was very tiny when she first came
to live with us.
So cute and funny we did make a lot
of fuss.

Perhaps we overdid it a bit and that's
why she's rather cross.
She parades around with head held
high, she thinks she is the boss.

Or it maybe when she had an accident
and got hit by a car.

It seemed to change her character, it
left a mental scar.

She grew and grew alarmingly and
was quite a sight to behold.
Her lovely grey fur expanded and her
flesh hung down in folds.

Our visitors would exclaim, "Oh what
a pretty cat!"
But when they bent to stroke her I'd
shout, "Oh don't do that!"

"I know she's sitting pretty but you
really must not be fooled.
One lightening swipe and your blood
would soon be pooled."

One day I'd made a birthday cake for
someone else to buy.
I left the room for a moment, I can't
remember why.

But when I returned I found that Cleo
was tucking in.

I was completely horrified and didn't
know where to begin.

What cat eats cake? With jam and
icing too!
Well apparently Cleo… she'd had a
bite or two.

I pushed Cleo out of the window, and
Cleo promptly threw up.
So now she'd made another mess that
I would have to clean up.

I salvaged the cake and patched it up,
it soon looked good enough.
Cleo drank two bowls of water then
disappeared, presumably to sleep it
off!

I think she learnt her lesson, she never
ate cake again.
Though she never lost any weight,
she only seemed to gain.

Four Cats, Three Tails

We have four cats but only three tails,
Three tall and straight and one just a
stump,
Poor Stanley had an accident,
And now has a rather odd rump.

Stanley had an accident,
We don't how it happened, we don't
know what he did,
Perhaps it was a speeding car,
When it went into a skid.

Poor Stanley had an accident,
And the vet was pretty sure,
He wouldn't use his tail again,
And he couldn't offer a cure.

Poor Stanley had an accident.
His tail was numb and limp,
He was being very brave,
You couldn't call him a wimp.

Poor Stanley had an accident,

He wasn't in any pain,
So we waited very patiently, though it
was all in vain.
His beautiful little tail would never
point up again!

Poor Stanley had a accident,
And went back to the vet.
He convalesced a week or two, he
couldn't go out yet.
But when he did…he proudly
revealed…
The cutest little butt!

One Moonlit Night

I looked at my lawn one fine sunny morn,
To my dismay it looked rather forlorn.
The bright green grass was not smooth
anymore,
Whatever had caused it I was ready for
war!!

There were tufts and divots all over the
place,
My beautiful lawn was in fact a disgrace.
We don't have a dog and the cats
wouldn't scrat.
Whatever could have happened to have
caused all that?

So I brushed away the soil and on the
divots I did stamp,
At this rate my lawn would soon need a
re-vamp.
But I just couldn't believe that the very
next day,
My lawn had been damaged in exactly the
same way.

Well this couldn't go on I was just not
having it.
So that night I watched through my
window to see what was doing it.
I sat in the dark staring out into the night.
The moon was full so the garden was
quite bright.

All of a sudden the security light came on,
I was amazed at what my eyes fell upon.
Who would have thought it in the middle
of my garden,
But there was the culprit, if you pardon!

His black nose twitched as he saw me
there,
He turned and ran, I must have given him
a scare.
It was the biggest creature in my garden I
have seen.
But he looked so scared that I felt a bit
mean.

I followed with my torch to see how he
got in,
But when I reached the fence there was no
sign of him.
Only a small gap that was his only escape.
How he got through it only left me agape.

So the very next day I filled in the gap,
And never again did I see the little chap.
I felt sad that I had blocked his way,
You don't see a badger in your garden
every day.

The Cat of Hay on Wye

He is black and white and lives in
Hay,
And hangs out in the Granary Café for
most of the day.
His name is Bracken but the waitress
calls him Bob,
Customer relations, that's his job.

He looks the part with his black coat
and white bib,
He wanders around cutting quite a jib.
The customers love him as he
welcomes them in.
He enjoys any tit bits
that are given to him.

He will sit by the fire enjoying the
warmth,
Sitting a while by the old fashioned
hearth.
The window sill is a good place to
stretch,

Waiting for new customers, he likes to
keep watch.

At the end of the day when his work is
done,
He says his goodbyes and heads off
home.
After a hearty supper and a good
night's sleep,
He'll be up early, as he has an
important role at The Granary to keep.

The Feline

The feline is quite sublime,
She'll glance at you if she's the time.
Maybe give a half smile,
As she lingers awhile.
A feline is quite sublime.

She'll rub by your foot,
But one move and she'll scoot.
As she slinks past, tail high,
You will wonder why,
A feline is quite sublime.

She is full of such grace,
With a beautiful face.
A shine on her fur,
And a soothing purr.
A feline is quite sublime.

She'll point her nose in the air,
As she makes for her chair.
How long she will dwell,
It is hard to tell.
A feline is quite sublime.

She may raise an eye,
At the buzz of a fly,
Then stretch out a paw,
Just to inspect a claw.
A feline is quite sublime.

Eyes like an owl,
For when she is out on the prowl,
To pounce on her prize,
She is so awfully wise.
A feline is quite sublime.

As she waits for her meal,
She will let you feel,
And as you stroke and pause,
You know that she's yours.
The feline is quite sublime.

HEALTH STUFF

Climate Change

Is it me or is it warm in here?
It must be the climate change that's
getting near.

It never used to be so hot at night,
Even when outside the world is white.

Is it me or is it warm in here?
The scientists must have it right, I
fear!

The thermostat is set to low,
But still I feel as if I glow.

In the office everyone else seems cool,
While I could use a dip in a pool.

Is it me or is it warm in here?

It must be Climate Change that makes
me feel this way,
Though no one else seems to notice, I
must say.

But now I'm at that certain age,
perhaps it *is* just me,
Is it Climate change? I'll just have to
wait and see.

Is it me or is it warm in here?

Hanging on to Me Marbles!

Oh me aching old bones!
They groan and shout at the start of
the day,
Till I've woken them up in the usual
way.
But at least I've got all me marbles!

Oh me aching old bones!
They tend to set if I sit too long,
They're getting weak when they used
to be strong.
But please don't let me lose me
marbles.

Oh me aching old bones!
I flop in a chair with a groan,
And get out of bed with a moan.
But I'm sure I've still got me marbles.

Oh me aching old bones!
When I kneel on the floor,
I can hardly get up any more.
But I *think* I've got *most* of me
marbles.

Oh me aching old bones!
How my spine creaks when I bend,
What *will* I be like in the end?
Especially if I've lost all me marbles.

Introduction to Yoga

Some people think that Yoga is tying
yourself in a knot,
But that simply isn't true, it just a load
of rot!
It's mainly a lot of stretching, that gets
you into shape,
And healthy eating of course and not
so much cake.

There are lots of different positions to
stretch your body out,
That wont get you hot and sweaty and
make your muscles shout.
There's The Dog and The Cat, The
Camel and The Crocodile,
You could be doing them *all* in just a
little while.

There is no competition, you go at
your own pace,
You could go to a class or practice at
your place.

You just need a book, a mat and a
room to your self,
A little gentle music and a candle on
the shelf.

Shut yourself in and let yourself go.
You'll be feeling relaxed before you
know.
Breath into the postures and clear the
mind.
It's so therapeutic, I think you will
find.

So when you've had a practise at all
the different postures,
You may even find that you'll never
need the Doctors.
Your mind will be relaxed and your
body so supple,
You may find yourself in The Lotus
without any trouble!

Keeping Cheerful

Life can be so busy, it's sad.
It's easy to forget the good times
we've had.

When we are having a stressful day,
It's sometimes hard to find our way.

Just stop and remember there's always
tomorrow.
And maybe you won' t feel too much
sorrow.

When you're stuck inside and feeling
gloomy,
Go for a walk where it's much more
roomy.

Read a book and get away from it all,
Eat some chocolate, however small.

If things get too much and you want to
drop out,

Lock yourself in the loo and have a
good shout!

So when you're feeling down in the
dumps,
Just be glad you haven't got mumps!

Man Flu

Man Flu…a very serious condition, or
so they would have you believe,
Copious amounts of sympathy, is
what they hope to achieve.
Women get it too,
But they don't call it flu.
It's something that they cope with and
just carry on with what they do.

But Man Flu is quite different and
just drives them to their bed,
When usually its nothing more than a
simple cold in the head.
They'll stay there for days and feel
sorry for themselves
Rows of different medicines lined up
on their shelves.

Women just leave Man to it.
Sympathy? Not a bit.
They sort the house and the children,
even go to work.

34

Life carries on, duties fulfilled,
Woman will never shirk.

Who else would look after the family,
the house and all the rest,
They may feel rough, and tired and
limp but they still do their best.
While Man lies recovering in his bed,
Even thinking that soon he could be
dead....
...of Man Flu?!!

Moonwater
(With meditation in mind)

It was moonlight as she walked to the
lake,
She had to do something for her own
sake.
She was troubled and scared,
Alone, no-one cared.

On the edge of the lake she stood and
gazed,
At the reflection of the moon, her
hand raised.
She felt the pull of the moon, drawing
her in.
Silently diving through the surface
and within.

She awoke on a shore of a sandy
white beach,
Nothing around her, not within reach.
A forest behind her, calling,
enchanting.

She ran to it, her breath panting.

Inside, cool and dark, underfoot soft
moss.
Trees all around, ahead paths cross.
Running water sounds came to her
ear.
At the next path she felt she was near.

A waterfall was now in sight,
A beautiful lady all in white.
Beckoned her silently to come to the
edge.
To sit beside her on a stony ledge.

Reaching into the water, pulling out a
black stone.
She bade her to follow, hers was white
as bone.
It was placed on her forehead, she felt
it's power.
Inside her head like the opening of a
flower.

The power flowed through her, she
became calm.
The bone white stone began to feel
warm.
Dropping it gently into the water,
flowing.
Once again she felt herself falling.

She travelled through space.
As light as soft gossamer lace.
Waking in her bed at home,
Ready for a new dawn.

My Big Toe

I think I've broken me toe.
I was only practising yoga, you know.
The posture I was doing was Salute to
the Sun
On all fours, pointing skyward was
my bum.
Well I took a great lunge
With my left leg did plunge.
And that's when we heard the snap!

Well I think I've broken me toe
I thought yoga was really good for
you, you know.
Well I did carry on for a bit,
Never thought I could've broken it.
But the pain didn't stop
And I only could hop.
Then the colours began to bloom.

I think I've broken me toe,
It was a simple movement you know
But my toe caught on my mat,

And that was that.
It began to swell
So I iced it for a spell
Hoping that would do the trick.

I think I've broken me toe,
There's nothing to be done, you know.
You just keep the ice on it,
And it helps if you can elevate it.
Otherwise you just grin and bear it.
And I though yoga kept you fit!
OUCH! I think I've broken me toe!

The Diet

To diet is a must, I fear,
But as Christmas is close I will wait
till next year.
In January there are still goodies
galore,
So it will have to wait a little bit more.

When February arrives, there are still
chocolates left.
Its Valentines Day, more chocolate I
suspect!
Next month is my birthday, a cake is a
must,
So I'll wait a bit longer, but soon I
trust.

Along comes April and Easter time
too,
I'll expect more chocolate, wouldn't
you?
But when the eggs are all gone,
I will diet or I will weigh a ton!

Weather is warmer now that May is
here,
Lots of salads, of chocolate keep
clear.
At the end of the month there's a
holiday,
So the diet will have to go by the way.

June comes in with lots of sun,
Eating salads I have begun.
July is full of social events,
Barbeques… so the diet went!

August brings the holiday season,
And eating out, I see no reason,
Eating cakes and ice-creams has to be
done,
A diet would only spoil all the fun!

September is a new beginning,
Diet I must if I want to get thinning.
Salad and yoghurt and cottage cheese,
Oh for a little chocolate pleeease.

It's getting chilly in October,

I'll have to sort out my pullover.
I find it hard to eat diet food,
When the weather is cold I can't be
good.

Now its November and really cold,
I can hide the flab under my jumpers
fold.
It will soon be Christmas with lots of
good cheer,
So I think the diet can wait till next
year!

SEASONAL STUFF

End of Summer

Nights darker, days shorter, holiday
memories now in the past.
But not to worry as Christmas is
looming fast.
Trees sparse, gardens bare, golden
leaves everywhere,
The smell of bonfires in the air.

Halloween Night, trick or treat,
Children knocking to beg some
sweets.
Scary masks on little faces,
Little hands waving plastic axes.

November the fifth,
Whiz, bang, pop!
They go on all night,
I wish they'd stop.

The heating is on, the curtains are
drawn,
All inside, cosy and warm.

Christmas is coming,
Better start planning!

Who's cooking the turkey,
Who's having to travel,
Huge list of presents,
For to unravel.

The month of January can be dull,
So choose a hobby or go for a ramble.
Lots of jobs that can be done,
While sitting waiting for summer to
come.

It's sad to leave the summer behind,
But changing seasons, clears the mind.
As soon as winter's come and gone.
We can start planning the summer's
fun!

Gardening

Weeding and bending, in the garden,
Pruning and stretching, in the garden,
Digging and heaving, in the garden,
Planting and kneeling, in the garden.
Tidy garden!

Back aching from bending,
Shoulders stiff from stretching,
Hands sore from digging,
Knees creaking from kneeling.
Pretty garden!

Trimming the lawn is easier,
Cutting the edges is tedious,
Pulling out the daisies, what a pain,
And watering when we have no rain.
Beautiful lawn!

Pots on the patio,
Lillies in the pond,
Wind rustling the bamboo,
Lights twinkling at dusk.
Magical garden!

Sitting in the garden,
When the work is done,
Enjoying all the flowers,
Sweet aromas in the air.
My garden.

Mevagissey

In the height of the summer it
becomes very busy,
Down on the harbour of Cornish
Mevagissey.
Pleasure boats and fishing boats
clambering for a mooring,
Flashy yachts and lobster pots freshly
filled that morning.

Crowds of people, pushchairs and
dogs.
An old sea dog looking for sea fogs.
A strong smell of fish from the
harbour or a diner.
Freshly baked pasties, nothing could
be finer.

Greedy fat seagulls screeching over
head,
Waiting for a morsel of food, if only a
crust of bread.

Dripping ice creams in the heat,
Leaving puddles around the feet.

Tiny houses, narrow streets leading to
the sea.
Painted doors and window boxes,
pretty as can be.
Bright sunshine and sparkling sea.
That's Mevagissey by the sea!

Pest Control

Have you ever had a problem with
slugs in your garden?
Well, I'll tell you about mine, if you'll
beg my pardon.
It took me years to realise what was
happening to my plants,
My marigolds would vanish, well, I
knew it wasn't the ants!

My Hostas had so many holes, they
looked as pretty as lace.
But there was no living thing in sight
and I looked all over the place.
I could see there was something
silvery, a slimy sort of trail,
Well that was probably only the
friendly garden snail.

Whatever it was that was eating my
plants they were eating them at night,
'Cos when I went out in the morning,
there wasn't a blighter in sight!

51

Now I was getting angry, throwing
money down the drain,
I would not buy any more plants just
for them to be eaten up again!

So, I did a bit of research and found
several things to try,
Eggshells was one and pellets I could
buy.
But pellets were very messy and just
left a pile of goo,
There must be something simpler,
what *was* I going to do?

Then I heard about a beer trap, that
sounded good to me,
You could get them from a mail order,
but that would cost a fee.
So I gathered empty jam jars and
bought a bottle of beer,
I poured a little in several and waited
for them to appear.

And sure enough they came in **droves**
to sample from the jar,

I was delighted to find my
expectations had been surpassed by
far!
They came from the four corners for
to take a sip,
And I scooped them up in a plastic
bag and sent them to the tip!

Scotland

The scenery in the highlands has to be
seen to be believed,
If I never saw it again I would be
sorely aggrieved.
The green hills rising from the depths
of a loch,
Changing in the sunlight as it moves
around the clock.
At dusk they are foreboding, looking
sinister in the dark.
There's not even a sound, if you
listen, hark?

The lochs are all around, glistening
through the trees,
Stretching through the forests and
there are many of these.
At the rise of every hill there is a
spectacular view.
I saw so many, yet still too few.
There are wide open spaces, only
grass and heather grow.

At a certain time of year the heathers
put on a purple show.

There are stone walls of castles, their
ruins still proud,
On the edge of a loch, under the mist
of a cloud.
Here battles were fought once, some
won and some lost.
Many thousands of warriors all
gathered in a host.
The history is colourful and yet times
were tragic.
But to stand on the ruins you can't
help feel the magic.

There are names we still know from
these battles of old.
To remind us of these men, there
stands in sun and cold,
Huge monuments of stone reaching
high into the sky.
They may not all have won, but how
they did try.

With their primitive weapons and
great heavy armour.
All of them fighting with great
strengths of valour.

The highlands islands are clustered
together,
Though often hidden in inclement
weather.
There's a bridge reaching over the
Kyle of Lochalsh,
That takes you to Skye, so beautiful,
what else,
Would you want on the Island of
Skye,
Such peace and tranquillity, Oh my!

Wide open spaces,
Where there are only traces
Of where ancient dwellings once
stood,
Made of stone with a roof of wood.
They were dragged from these crofts,

Leaving all of their crops

There stands a lone piper, a haunting
sound,
The sound of Scotland echo's all
around.
The tartan of each clan, of a different
name,
An individual pattern for each to
claim.
They have a share of the land to own,
Until it is taken and from it they're
thrown.

Return I must to the Scottish
Highlands so fair,
Maybe in winter when there is a chill
in the air.
The mountains of green would now be
all white,
Their snow covered peaks a
magnificent sight.
The highland cattle roaming free,

Wandering down for a drink from the
sea.

Their food is unique, the haggis is a
rare treat,
It's a strange combination with very
little meat.
It is served up in a variety of ways,
Mainly with tatties and neeps, it says.
The shortbread is good and full of
butter.
The finest of food, it couldn't be
better.

SCOTLAND!

Spring!

To hear the birds singing to welcome
the dawn,
You know it's the time to begin a new
morn.
The soft breeze wafting through the
open window,
Gently refreshes and you feel a warm
glow,
It's spring!

To look out of your window and see
down below,
How sharp the colour of the grass just
mown.
New plants and new shoots that
suddenly appear,
After lying dormant for half of the
year.
It's spring!

Vivid purple primulas, proud yellow
daffodils,

The blackbirds, worming, with bright
yellow bills.
Pink blossom on the trees so pretty in
the sun,
All herald that a new season has
begun.
It's spring!

The chill in the mornings and the
warmth in the day,
Make us aware that the summer is on
its way.
Doves in the evening cooing to their
mate,
As the sun begins setting when it's not
yet late.

It's spring!

The Great British Summer

Hazy days, lazy days,
The Great British Summer!

Blue skies, fluffy clouds,
The Great British Summer!

Hot sun, cool shade,
The Great British Summer!

Sun hats, no coats,
The Great British Summer!

Short shorts and sun cream,
The Great British Summer!

Balmy evenings, humid nights,
The Great British Summer!

Storms by night, sun by day,
The Great British Summer!

Faces smiling, people happy,
The Great British Summer!

Perfect weather, perfect place,
Britain in summer!

Who Moved the Mountains?

Who moved the mountains?
They looked so majestic, only
yesterday,
With the sun glinting on the snow,
As we came past this way.

Who moved the mountains?
Today there is no sign of where they
used to be.
Even the loch seems to be fading,
It all seems very strange to me.

Who moved the mountains?
They were such a sight to behold,
And the loch sparkling in the sun,
Just as beautiful as I had been told.

Who moved the mountains?
It's all so mysterious, I so want to see
them again.
And the loch is barely visible,
Maybe it's to do with the rain!

Who moved the mountains?
Will they ever be returned.
And the loch in all its glory,
Oh how I have yearned.

Who move the mountains?
What is the shadow in the distance?
Could it be the mountains?
I do believe I caught a glimpse.

Who moved the mountains?
Well…they haven't been moved at all.
There they are, appearing through the
clouds,
It must have been just the heavy rain
fall.

Winter

The winter landscape is black and
white,
Its dull and dreary, not a welcoming
sight.
The wind is howling throughout the
night,
The rain beats down with all it's
might.

The trees are bending in the force of
the gale,
The windows are battered in a deluge
of hail.
Wild animals hibernate curled up in
their tail,
Small boats moored, too choppy to
sail.

Trees like skeletons without their
leaves,
Small birds hiding high in the eaves.

Bulbs in the ground, waiting to
receive,
Some warmth from the sun for which
it grieves.

The days are so short and the nights
are so long,
Unlike the summer when the days are
so long.
Heads are bent down when walking
along,
Hurrying home to wherever they
belong.

The world turns white when snow
begins to fall,
Coating all the treetops, short and tall,
Covering the garden, piled high on the
wall,
Softening the sounds, even the birds
call.

Owls in the barn with their head under
their wing,

All is waiting for what a new season
may bring.
When the birds will return and begin
to sing.
But now all is dormant and waiting for
Spring.

FOOD STUFF

'Twas the Night Before……..

'Twas the night before grocery day
and all through the house,
No food could be found, not a crumb
for a mouse.

Barely enough milk for our cocoa that
night,
We opened the tin, not a biscuit in
sight!

The fridge was near empty, the bread
gone quite stale,
Must get to Tesco tomorrow without
fail!

In a bowl on the table, looking
awfully sad,
One brown banana and an apple gone
bad.

We checked all the cupboards for
something to snack,

Was that a Pot Noodle hiding there at
the back?

Yes there was a Pot Noodle but it was
well past it's date,
So we shared a stale crust, my
goodness, what a state!

We shared a cup of cocoa, there
wasn't any more,
Roll on tomorrow when we can get to
the store.

Coffee Drinkers Dilemma!

Quick cup of coffee from a coffee
shop,
Used to be quite simple, but now it's
not!

So many options, not just black or
white!
Dozens of choices they create such a
plight.

The waitress reels them off a such a
great speed,
Just a cup of coffee, please, is all I
need.

Flat white, Latte, black or
cappuccino?
Decaf, long black, skinny or
Americano?

Gingerbread Latte, salted caramel, or
Espresso?
Mocha, Macchiato, or even Affogato?

Well I'm sure I don't know!

So I make my choice but it's not over
yet!
Even more choices for a coffee for to
get.

So many different sizes and they're all
quite large,
Small, regular, medium or large?

Milk, cream or skinny, which would I
prefer?
Anything will do, I just want my
coffee to sit and stir!

Cup of coffee and a Slice of Cake

Don't you just love a nice cup of
coffee and a slice of cake?
A trip into town to meet an old friend,
You do a little shopping but always at
the end,
There'll be a nice cup of coffee and a
slice of cake!

Off to the garden centre to buy new
plants,
Or maybe for treatment to get rid of
the ants.
But you know where you'll stop for a
little break,
For a nice cup of coffee and a slice of
cake!

Even on a long trip when you go out
for the day,

You'll be looking for a stop off when
you're about halfway.
A little country tea shop where they
do all home bake,
To enjoy a nice cup of coffee and a
slice of cake!

A visit to a stately home with gardens
for to roam,
There's always that last place before
you go home.
It's the coffee shop in the boathouse
overlooking the lake,
Where you relax and enjoy, a nice cup
of coffee and a slice of cake!

A fund raising event is always good to
do,
Donating money and having fun too.
Meeting friends and neighbours and
taking a break,
Where you're sure to get a nice cup
coffee and a slice of cake!

Healthy Living?

Fish and chips, sausage and mash,
Bacon and eggs and corned beef
hash,
A staple diet for years gone past.

Groaty pud, faggots and peas,
To eat this lot you'd be down on
your knees.
Not so good now, if you please.

Salad and pasta, no meat or fat,
Is apparently healthy, what do you
think of that?
No fat, no sugar, no taste. What?

Bread pudding, suet pudding, rice
pudding with jam.
Great big spoonful's into your
mouth you'd cram.
Now it's fruit smoothies that leave
you still fam.

"A little of what you fancy," said my
old Nan.
"All things in moderation," if only
you can!
Apparently we all should have a
Healthy Eating Plan.

Well I have a balanced diet, I think
I've got it right,
I weigh out all my chocolates and
cakes, such a tempting sight.
Then I equal it with fruit and veg
and create my balanced diet!

Marmite

Marmite is an acquired taste,
A thick brown sticky
paste.

Spread it on
your toast,
Spread it on a roast.
Put it in a stew,
To name but a few.

If you really
like it spread it on
thick,
If you really hate it, it could
make you sick.

It's a love or
hate thing, I think
you'll agree.
Do *you* love it or hate
it?

I love it! But that's just me!

The Buffet

We all love a buffet, free food for all,
Whatever the occasion, we all have a
ball!
Eighteen, twenty one, forty or sixty,
And if your really lucky right up to
eighty!
Could be romantic, a Wedding or
Engagement,
An Anniversary or a Christening or
any other sentiment.

They'll all have a buffet of that you
can be sure,
Carefully wrapped in tin foil, that'll be
the lure.
What lies beneath the wrappings, will
remain hidden.
Peeping or sampling is strictly
forbidden!
Set out on a table at the end of the
room,

Everyone keeps glancing, it must be
unveiled soon!

At last the time is come and it all
looks very grand,
Everyone is lining up with a plate in
their hand.
It's really quite a banquet, with food
to suit all tastes,
They pile it on, as much as they can,
it's far too good to waste.
The queue moves round the table, as
slowly as they can,
Not wanting to miss any tasty morsels,
that were delivered in a van.

We all get so excited but it's nearly
always the same,
Sausage rolls of course, because of
their fame.
Cheese rolls, ham rolls and maybe a
little beef,

All garnished neatly with tomato and
a little green leaf.
Potato salad, coleslaw and things on
sticks.
Even spicy things that not everyone
picks.

There at the end, are desserts that you
can't yet touch,
But once they are opened there'll be
such a rush.
The gateaux is still frozen, but gets
eaten anyway,
The profiteroles were scrumptious,
everyone will say.
Then comes the celebration cake and
the lights go dim,
Happy Birthday is sung for her or for
him.

The buffet table stands all alone, and
is looking rather grim.
Not at all like the beginning with all
its fancy trim.

The rolls have fallen apart and their
contents all dried up,
They no longer look good enough
even for a pup.
There's nuts in the coleslaw and the
edges of that are crusty,
The left over pickled onions have
made the silver rusty.

Everyone is leaving now, and the
buffet looks so sad,
Once it looked so wonderful, but a
good time was had.
Some people wrap up left overs, in a
serviette or bag,
I think we'll leave that plate, there's
the end of a fag!
It was a lovely celebration, of that we
all know,
But I think that the Buffet was the star
of the show!

The Haggis

Haggis is a bit like Marmite, an
acquired taste, of course.
But try it, it's delicious when its
smothered in Whisky sauce.

You can eat it the traditional way,
with just the tatties and neaps,
Or on a burger with the haggis piled
on top in heaps!

It may not look inviting, but please
don't be too hasty,
Give it a try, it's got some bite and is
extremely tasty.

In Scotland they like to serve it up it
many different ways,
Variety is the spice of life and variety
usually pays.

It's often served with chicken, in one
way or another,

So why not get the recipe and try it on
your mother!

The oddest one without a doubt was
haggis on a pizza,
But even so it wasn't bad and had a
wonderful aroma.

The best of course is with the Whisky
sauce,
That you could eat without *any* force!

LIFE STUFF

Full of Beans!

You know that saying "full of beans'.
Well where does it come from, what
does it mean?

After all these years of wondering, I
think I've just found out.
In our little granddaughter, who's
forever leaping about!

She used to go to ballet class, but she
found it too sedate,
I realise now that it must have been
the amount of beans she ate!

She comes to tea on Mondays and
when I ask her what she wants for tea?
I know the answer already, she'll say
"Can I have beans for tea?"

It may be with her fish fingers, or
nuggets or whatever she's tried,

It may be just some toast or a
sandwich, but it's always beans on the
side!

She goes to dance class now and can
throw herself around,
But even that is not enough to use up
her energy abound.

I've always thought a gym class
would be right up her street,
Where she could run and jump and
throw herself off her feet.

So we make sure she is full of beans
to keep her energy levels high,
For leaping off the springboard and
soaring towards the sky!

Grandparents

When the next generation comes
along,
Memories flood back of when your
own were young.
But it's not the same as you soon find
out,
It's even more fun and you rarely need
to shout.

They come to stay for the afternoon,
The visit is over far too soon.
You've played with the toys and read
a book,
They point with a finger and say
"Grandad, look!"

The best is when you get out the old
toys,
That were kept in the loft for the next
girls and boys.
You tell them that "Mummy once
played with this",

And you're sure it will be a favourite
of his.

There's a few old books that have
been kept on the shelf,
Which you will read till they can read
for themself.
When you are babysitting and there all
night,
You can take your time to tuck them
in tight.

They are a shining light that come into
your life,
And you don't get all the trouble and
strife.
But when they get a handful and
you've had enough,
You can take them home for the
parents to get tough!

I'm a Pensioner

I never used to be outspoken, I was always
rather quiet,
But now if I am crossed, I am ready to start a
riot!
After years and years of holding it in,
I have earned the right to try and win!
I'm a pensioner!

I would always wait quite patiently when
standing in a queue,
Let people push in, but only a few.
But now as I stand firm my ground,
There's no chance *anyone* will get around.
I'm a pensioner!

Waiting at the bus stop, brandishing my bus
pass,
Stepping in front of the young ones, they're
now *second* class.
They may glare and shake their head.
But I turn and smile....enough said!

I'm a pensioner!

When I got those phone selling window
frames and such,
I would listen quite politely and not say very
much.
But now when they ask me if I have a moment
or two,
I reply, "Who wants to know? or "Who the
hell are you?"
I'm a pensioner!

When I had been out shopping and a purchase
was not quite right,
I'd just make do and let it go and think, "Oh
that's alright!"
But now I put my coat on and go back to the
shop,
And tell them "I'm *not* happy and I *won't* be
fobbed off!"
I'm a pensioner!

So getting older can be fun when you can
'have a go',

Getting stroppy and impatient comes with age,
you know!
All those years you've held your tongue, but
now you just let rip.
So don't hold back now, just let your mouth
unzip!
Be a pensioner!

Jumble Sale

A Jumble Sale?
What is that? The young may ask.
Well a pile of old clothes, it was quite
a task!

Modern name…. a Table Top sale.
No segregation and so much fun!
Open the doors and in they would run!

A dash to the trestles with a trip and a
stumble,
To get there first, how the floor would
rumble.
Push to the front to get a good fumble
Through the mountainous heaps of
assorted jumble.

They were usually held in the local
church hall,
Sometimes in spring and sometimes in
fall.

Grabbing and snatching through the
old men's knickers,
You never know, they could've been
the vicars!

Charity shops and car boots now serve
the same purpose,
Second hand clothes for some of the
workers.
Now it's so easy to search through
clothes on a rail,
But not nearly as much fun as a
JUMBLE SALE!

Mrs Dunn's Class

Mrs Dunn was waiting for the class to
settle down,
She waited very patiently but gave
them such a frown.
They were busy chatting and rolling
around the floor,
And didn't seem to notice the terrible
scowl that she wore.

Little Archie was under the table,
having a lovely time,
And Anna and Rosie were happily
doing some kind of rhyme.
Billy and Jack were saying how each
had spent their spends,
While Joey thought it great fun to
blow raspberries from both ends!

Mrs Dunn had had enough and
clapped her hands three times,
Most of them sat still now but still
there were several whines.

"Now listen children, this is just not
on, the lesson should begin,
"So now I want good listening or at
break you'll be kept in!"

So Mrs Dunn began, at last, her task
of teaching Class 2D,
But it wasn't going to happen, some
just wanted to be free.
Andrew starting drifting and picking
at his toes,
And David had his finger halfway up
his nose.

Wendy played with Izzie's hair and
styled it in a plait,
Alfie's got his finger stuck, how *did*
he manage that!
The raspberries had started up and
were coming thick and fast,
Would she ever get to teach them and
how long could she last?

At last she put a film on all about the
Guy Fawkes' Plot,

They even asked some questions
about why he should not be forgot.
She finally had their attention but it
was all in vain,
As the bell had sounded for break and
they were off again!!

My Dad

When I was young, he would take me
out,
If I did wrong he would never shout.
He taught me things I have never
forgot,
He even gave me a garden plot.
My Dad was always there!

When I was a teenager and out on the
town,
He would be a taxi without a frown.
On holidays I could take a friend,
I'm sure we drove him round the
bend!
My Dad was always there!

When I got married he gave me away,
It certainly was a happy day.
We bought a house of our very own,
He helped make it a home without a
moan.
My Dad was always there!

When our family increased and he
was a Grandad,
He was the best one that they could
have had.
A desk, a dolls house and a rocking
horse,
All made by Grandad, of course!
My Dad was always there!

When our children were small, and the
lawns got too long,
He'd be there with his lawnmower
and a song!
He would pull out the weeds and put
in some plants,
And know what to do if we had too
many ants!
My Dad was always there!

When our girls were at school and
needed a lift,
He'd gladly oblige and would never
be miffed.
He'd be at the school Fete and spend a
few pennies.

He'd even give them a game of tennis.
My Dad was always there!

When they grew up and had a home of
their own,
He would often help out and give
them a loan.
When he became slower than he used
to be,
He'd still have his great-grandson on
his knee.
My Dad was always there!

One day when had slowed right down,
He couldn't even make it to town.
I did his shopping to help him out,
He was pretty upset he could not get
about.
But my Dad was still there!

He went into hospital for some extra
care,
But never came back to sit in his
chair.
It's hard to believe he has really gone,

But sitting and thinking, the memories
come.
My Dad will always be there!
If only in my heart.

The Dinner Ladies

Standing on the playground,
There's mayhem all around.
Around the playground they patrol,
Already things look out of control.

Children racing to and fro.
Tag is played, one-two-three-Go!
Why is Stanley climbing the fence?
A dinner lady calls, come hence!

There's a collision in the middle,
One is hurt, the other just giggles.
The dinner lady helps him up,
The other one is off with a gallop.

The little knee is soon wiped clean,
He says his mate is being mean!
The dinner lady feels a tap,
It's Sophie saying she's had a slap!

The culprit now is out of sight,
But in the distance she can see a fight.
She strides across with book in hand,

Pointing at them to make them stand!

Billy says it wasn't him,
It was Harry who punched him on the
chin.
A crowd has gathered to tell the tale,
All that is heard is one big wail.

Names are entered in the book,
The dinner lady says, "Now look!
If you can't behave you'll be sent to
the Head."
Their faces changed to a look of
dread.

There are some children playing
nicely,
Singing songs and talking politely.
But Alfie is pulling Jennie's hair,
And someone's shoe is sailing through
the air.

The dinner lady sighs in disbelief,
But there goes the bell and what a
relief!

There's a stampede to get in the line,
Thank goodness that's the end of
dinnertime!

The One Man Band (The Busker)

His travelling days are over,
He can tell a tale or two.
The sights he's seen all over the land,
The Busker, The One Man Band.

Drum on his back, cap on head,
Guitar and harmonica in his hand.
He'd set up on the street, though
sometimes got banned,
The Busker, The One Man Band.

But he brought good cheer,
And the crowds would smile,
As he played his songs of his
particular brand.
The Busker, The One Man Band.

Across the seas, wherever he played,
His music was no language barrier,
People would stop and raise their
hands,
To the Busker, The One Man Band.

It wasn't just the coins he got,
He was given cans of beer,
A sandwich and a shake of the hand,
For the Busker, The One Man Band.

In Norway and in Germany,
He'd brave their winter weather,
He'd happily play his music for a long
as he could stand,
The Busker, The One Man Band.

But now he has his memories,
And dons his kit for fun,
He doesn't use it often but it always
near at hand,
The Busker, The One Man Band!

Wedding Made in...

The Bride was expecting so was really
quite large!
The in-laws were unkind, said she
looked like a barge.

The Groom wasn't much better, but he
was stick thin,
The in-laws said his beard could do
with a trim.

The day had been planned so all
would go well,
But with the unlikely union you
couldn't quite tell.

The Bridesmaids stood waiting all in a
row,
But even they themselves made quite
a show.

A plump one, a round one another
quite scraggy,

One dress was quite tight but one was
quite baggy.

The Best Man was huge and had a
black eye,
The in-laws again raised their eyes
with a sigh.

He got into a fight on the Stag Night
they think,
Probably because he'd had too much
to drink!

The service was rushed, the vicar
looked flushed.
He collapsed right after and to the
hospital was rushed!

The Photographer arrived with a patch
on one eye,
But he'd do his best, he promised to
try.

The Reception all ready and the room
looked quite nice.

The Guests arrived and it got wrecked
in a trice!

The balloons came down and there
was food on the floor,
The drinks got spilt so they got shown
the door.

The happy couple set off on their
honeymoon,
But the car broke down and they were
stranded soon.

So they stayed the night in a local pub,
A lumpy bed but plenty of grub.

Once more they set off in the hope of
some sun,
But out of the oven the bun decided to
come!

Widdershins

Widdershins is a weird word, and it
doesn't mean anything good!
Don't know if you've heard it,
There's no reason that you should.

It's got nothing to do with widows,
And nothing to do with shins!

Only heard it myself a month or two
ago,
So I'm going to try and explain it,
Just so that you know.

Widdershins…a weird word!
A superstition so I've heard.

It's a very ancient word, dates back to
pagan times,
In several different languages the
meaning is still the same.

It means to go backwards, against the
sun,
When clockwise is the way it should
be done.

Widdershins can mean bad luck if you
don't follow the rule,
Not anti clockwise around a church,
clockwise is the rule.

If you Widdershins several times you
could end up in Elfland.
A child once did this round a church
and still he's not been found!

So if you should Widdershins you're
evoking trouble,
If you decide to Widdershins you
could summon up the devil!

MORE SERIOUS
STUFF

All Things Obsolete

We used to have to sit on one place to
make a phone call,
The telephone was often screwed to
the wall.
But now we have the mobile phone!

You used to have an alarm clock that
would wake you up,
Often a loud ringing bell telling you
its time to get up.
But now we have the mobile phone!

Everyone had a camera to record
memorable events,
Birthday parties, family pets and
holidays in tents.
But now we have the mobile phone!

Diaries were a must to remember
future dates,

Like meetings and birthdays and a
drink with your mates.
But now we have the mobile phone!

A calendar on the wall so you could
plan ahead,
So you didn't have to worry about
keeping dates in your head.
But now we have the mobile phone!

Letter writing is a thing of the past,
E.mails and texting, technology
moves too fast.
Cos now we all have a mobile phone!

A calculator to do your sums,
To work out how to pay your bills.
But now we have a mobile phone!

Information was found in an
encyclopaedia,
Google is the answer, it's all there for
the media.
All you ever need is on your mobile
phone!

On a long distance trip you would
need a map,
Now into the phone a post code you
tap.
A Sat. Nav is built into your mobile
phone.

So many things we don't do anymore,
So may things we don't need
anymore.
And it's all because of the mobile
phone!

Flame

A flame is such a little thing,
It can be strong and powerful in it's
own way.
It can light a candle,
A circle of light to help you on your
way.

A hundred little flames,
All burning at the same time,
Could light up a Great Hall,
A castle or cathedral in olden times.

A tiny flame can become ferocious,
If not kept in check.
It can start a blaze so devastating,
Destroy a forest, a building it could
wreck.

But one little flame,
Can be romantic,
All at the same time,

If lighting up a table over a bottle of
wine.

A tiny flame could burn in your heart,
If you were filled with desire,
In search of your one true love,
Of your heart's desire.

So light your flame with caution,
Don't underestimate it's power.
It could light up your life for a
moment,
But ruin it within an hour!

Morning Stroll - A Protest

Walking down the street and what do I
see?
Nothing unusual it seems to me.
There's morning traffic rushing by.
A honking horn, an impatient guy.
A screech of brakes, lights on red.
What a maniac, what's in his head?

Walking down the street and what do I
see?
A cacophony of sound it seems to me!
Kids off to school, trailing coats and
bags,
Mothers with pushchairs smoking
fags.
Don't they realize the damage they
do....
Not just to themselves but to their
children too.

Walking down the street and what do I
see?
A lot of selfish people it seems to me.

117

Lollipop lady in the middle of the
road,
Enormous lorry with a heavy load,
Too late to stop! The lady cringes,
Missed the lollipop by just a few
inches.

Walking down the street and what do I
see?
A lot of chaos it seems to me.
A cyclist wearing all the right gear,
But that van is cutting him up I fear!
The blare of a horn, the shake of a fist,
The van speeds away in a cloud of
exhaust mist.

Walking down the street and what do I
see?
People being thoughtless it seems to
me.
Pushchair and wheelchair users full of
wrath,
To find cars on pavements blocking
their path.
Dog mess left for a child to tread in,

118

Even though on the corner there's a
doggy bin!

Walking down the street and what do I
see?
A bad way to start the day it seems to
me.
So much anger all around,
Why can't everyone just slow down.
They'd feel much better by the end of
the day,
If only they'd realize there's another
way.

The Black Country

The sound of the hammer rang out
And the stamp came down with a
clout.
A mighty thud could be heard in the
day,
A rhythm to be heard all the way.

In the heat and the dust and the
dimness,
Men toiled with their shirt sleeves
rolled up.
You could see the red glow of the
great lengths of steel,
As they sweated from breakfast till
sup.

Every street corner had its own little
pub,
Where the workmen would go after a
jolly good scrub.

They would down their ale and each
tell a tale,
Till they all went back home to hear
their wives wail.

The women would be working just as
hard,
Cooking and cleaning and sweeping
the yard.
With their overalls on and a turban on
their head,
They would feed all the children and
put them to bed.

Even then there was still work to be
done,
Polishing the brasses until they shone.
Mending and darning and bringing in
the coal,
They never complained, it was part of
their role.

On market days the towns would be
packed,

Stalls would be plentiful, nothing
lacked.
All that you needed would be right on
hand,
No need to go searching all over the
land.

Milk was delivered right to your door.
You'd just leave a note if you needed
more.
Fresh fruit and veg and a loaf of
bread,
All came in a van for the family to get
fed.

The weekend arrived and they'd be
down at the track,
The smell of the fuel as the bikes
raced back.
'Ommer 'em Cradley' you would hear
them shout.
At the end of the night, they'd call in
for a stout.

Canals cutting through, passing
factory walls.
A colourful barge, through a tunnel it
crawls.
Pulled by a horse, huge and strong.
The lock keeper watches all day long.

It has its history, a Deer Park and
Castle, grand.
Stately homes in acres of land,
With fountains and lakes glistening in
the sun.
Where birds and wild animals aplenty
would run.

It's much different now with the castle
in ruins,
And the Deer Park covered with
several buildings.
Although some of the changes I think
are quite wrong,
The Black Country is where I grew up
and belong.

The Lady of Charlecote Park

Mary Elizabeth married a man that
was not her choice,
In the nineteenth century she had no
voice.
She fell in love with his home on
sight,
And there soon was a bond with him
that was so tight.

Charlecote Park was a wonderful
place,
But soon she began to change its face.
She was now a Lucy and Mistress of
the house,
A Lucy had lived there for years, she
wouldn't grouse.

Mary was kept busy with the house
and estate,
There was always a task that just
wouldn't wait.
She took her part well as the Lady of
the Manor

And all that she did was conducted
with valour.

The next generation began to arrive,
Several children but not all would
survive.
There was a terrible sadness that hung
over Charlecote,
But 'Life carries on," is an appropriate
quote.

They travelled abroad for two years or
more,
When they'd lost a young baby and
Mary's heart tore.
On their return with their hearts full of
joy,
For they now had with them their new
baby boy.

Mary wanted the house to look even
more grand,
So the moved into a cottage on the
edge of their land.

It was a major task and seven long
years it took,
To give Charlecote Park a much
grandeur look.

The years passed by and the family
grew,
Still more sadness if only she knew.
But Mary was a lady of such inner
strength,
And managed to keep buoyant at
whatever length.

Sadly her husband passed on quite
young,
She nursed him to the end and had to
be strong.
Her grandchildren came and she
helped them delivered,
Quite unexpected but our Mary never
quivered.

Mary Elizabeth had led a long and full
a life.

She had built a new church, through
trouble and strife,
Where several of her family were
already laid.
A rose window for George, her late
husband she bade.

She was well into her seventies and
still entertained,
With parties and music, much
admiration was gained.
She still played her harp and could
dance well too,
Then wrote all her memories for her
family to view.

When her eldest son married and took
him wife,
She handed over Charlecote, it was a
big change in her life.
Although she was no longer the Lady
of Charlecote Park,
She lived out her days there, it was so
dear to her heart.

What's it all about?

What's it all about?
I'm sure I don't know!
I don't understand politics and
different religions.
But innocent people being shot or
maimed,
Won't solve anything.

What's it all about?
I'm sure I don't know!
Suicide bombers blowing themselves
to bits.
What do they think it will prove?
They're only another number to the
death toll.

What's it all about?
I'm sure I don't know!
People killing people all across the
world.
Always the innocent who suffer most.
Wasted lives, nothing changes.

What's the answer?
I'm sure I don't know!
You'd think by now there'd be a
solution,
But no, it's always another revolution.
Do we have to live our life in terror?
Will there be changes or is this
forever?

EVERY DAY STUFF

Guest Speaker

The 'Ladies That Do Lunch' club was
going very well.
Numbers were increasing, that's how
we could tell.
The caterers we hired always did us
proud,
Even offered veggie meals for those
that meat wasn't allowed.

Our ladies so looked forward to our
monthly gathering.
Bought new hats and booked their
perms, and picked out all their bling.
Phone calls made to arrange their
transportation,
Guessing the speaker and hoping it
would meet their expectation.

The last few after-dinner speakers had
been disappointing of late,
There's only so much you can take in
about an ancient cracked old plate.

There was a little more interest in
Tutankhamen's Tomb,
But then the next one was so full of
doom and gloom.

Now the ladies were despondent, and
getting rather bored .
They needed something stimulating,
something new, they had implored.
So Betty searched for new ideas, in
magazines and on the net.
Till she came up with a solution and
knew just who she'd get.

Well ladies of a certain age can
sometimes let things go,
So keeping healthy and in shape
would be lesson to know.
His name was Bernie Slick, his
nickname "Mr Fit".
He could show the ladies a few things
from which they all could benefit.

The lunch had been devoured and they
were ready to be entertained.

Betty hoped Bernie would be here
soon before their attention waned.
In he came and scanned the room, a
frown upon his face.
It looked as if he thought he may be in
the wrong place.

However, Betty put him straight and
welcomed him into the throng.
She pointed to the podium and
introduced him before too long.
The ladies all sat waiting with a look
of anticipation,
They were hoping to find out how to
achieve a body of perfection.

There was a little hush as Bernie stood
before them,
He switched his CD player on and
waited for it to begin.
The music was quite lively, it had a
good dance beat,
The ladies were enjoying it and all
began tapping their feet.

Bernie began his movements, but
never uttered a word,
His arms went up, his legs went out,
his arms flapped like a bird.
He went in to a starling spin, his
jacket flew clean off.
The ladies thought that this was odd,
could this be a rip-off.
Bernie was really moving now in a
very energetic way,
He looked at the ladies with a leer, as
he began to sway.
A leap in the air and then down on his
knees, his trousers in his hand.
Well Betty gasped, Gladys paled and
needed to be fanned.

The ladies now were in quite a state
and didn't know where to look,
As Bernie stood in his sheepskin
thong and realised he'd been mistook.
Betty hurried over and ushered him
out with a huff.
Saying, "Thank you very much but I
think we've seen enough!

New Sofa

We went to look at sofas, just the
other day,
There was such a sea of sofas, I
couldn't find my way.
A Salesman came to greet us with a
smile upon his face,
Asking if he could help to guide us
around the massive place.

We told him we were browsing and
didn't intend to buy,
But we could tell by the look on his
face, he was going to give it a try.
He asked what we were looking for,
well we didn't really know,
I looked around the store, there were
so many of them on show.

He pointed out the offers that were
just too good to miss,
He even introduced himself and said
his name was Chris.

"Here's one you just must try, the
comfort is second to none,"
So we sat on it and bounced a bit,
could this be the one?

But we had hardly started, there were
loads more yet to try,
In this store and several more before
we were to buy.
We gathered all the info and Chris
was very helpful,
Though a lot of what he told us was
all a load of bull!

We got back home with our brochures
of prices fabrics and such,
We couldn't make our mind up, we
had taken in so much.
I sat down on my sofa with a welcome
cup of tea,
And suddenly I realised. . .. .. this was
the only sofa for me!

Old Friend

It was gift to you from me,
That you found neatly wrapped under the
Christmas tree.
You opened it up with a smile on your
face,
And your gratitude was full of grace.
It fitted you snug,
Like a bug in a rug,
As you paraded about the place.

It was cosy and warm and zipped up to
your chin,
Just as you liked it, not bought on a
whim.
To find the right one I had searched near
and far,
It was lucky I had use of the car.
It was soft and dark blue,
When it was brand new.
It was the finest you'd had by far.

As the years rolled by it became a good
friend,
Even now at the very end.
You wear it with pride,
Though it looks like it died.

It's gone very thin and there's a hole or
two,
And the colour had faded as well.
But you won't let it go, oh no, not you!

A new one was given to replace the old,
And still you would not do as told!
You wear it all day doing jobs round the
house.
It looks like its been chewed, perhaps by
a mouse.
The sleeves have gone long,
And the back looks all wrong.
If I say any more you'll just grouse!

So please, I implore,
Chuck it out of the door.
I know it's a wrench
To sling in over the fence,
But it really does need to be done.
I huff and I puff,
It's been around long enough,
Your old blue cardigan.

Spoons

Where do all the teaspoons go?
It sure is a mystery that I don't know.
There's always that one at the bottom of the bowl,
Surely they don't go down the plug hole?

It's only the everyday ones that seem to go missing
Not the best ones for when people are visiting.
They only get used for stirring the tea,
But they get fewer and fewer, now there's only
three.

When I tidied the drawer I found one hiding,
But that was the only one there for the finding.
In the garage I found one covered in glue,
And one by the cat litter covered in…!

Well now we have six but that's not enough,
I could try the other drawer, that's full of stuff.
There must be a spoon thief that nicks them in the
night,
That's the only answer I've come up with for my
plight.

But if that's the case, why only take teaspoons?
Not the big ones like dessert or tablespoons.
They must be little people who can't carry a heavy
load,
If only I could catch them I would chase them
down the road.

Of course it must be the Borrowers who live
beneath the floor,
Whatever do they use them for and always wanting
more.
Well now I've got ten boxes... all hidden away,
They won't be getting these ones, oh never, not in
my day!

The Voice

Sitting in a restaurant making your
choice,
And then you hear it…the extremely
loud voice.

It drowns out all the other sounds and
penetrates your brain.
You know there'll always be one, it's
always the same.

You can't concentrate on the menu as
you hear about their life,
The worst of it is you know it's some
poor bloke's wife.
Or even a bloke with a long suffering
wife.

No matter how many people are in are
in their little group,
There's just this one loud voice that
keeps breaking through.

You never hear the questions, it's just
the answers that ring out.
You feel the tension building and you
feel you want to shout.

It could be a posh Bistro or a local
little café,
There's sure to be that one person
that has a raucous laugh.

You'll hear about their shopping trips
and health issues too.
It really beings to feel as if the
speaking directly to you.

You try so hard to ignore them and
try to enjoy your meal.
But they have no idea of the intrusion
that you feel.

They continue with their jolly
chatting for all the world to hear,
While you really wish that they
weren't sitting quite so near.

The Waiting Game

Sitting in a waiting room waiting to
hear your name,
You're not alone there's several
people doing just the same.
You sit and smile politely and glance
at the walls around,
Reading all the notices but nothing
interesting is found.

You look for the clock and then
glance at your watch,
"That can't be right!" but yes they
both match.
You take a deep breath and try to stay
calm,
You take off your coat, it's getting a
little warm.

You look for a magazine on the little
coffee table,
But there's only Farmers ones of
horses and stables.

You look at the clock and then at your
watch,
And unfortunately they both do still
match.

People come and people go,
And you just sit there waiting to go!
There's so much at home that you
could be doing,
Than watch other people to-ing and
fro-ing.

Surely you must be called in soon,
You're the only one left in the waiting
room.
Sitting and waiting with your fist on
your chin.
Finally a door opens and you get
called in!

Trinkets and Tranklements

Trinkets and tranklements , what a
lovely sound,
Reminds of my Grandma with her bits
and pieces around.

You'll not find it in any dictionary,
I've already had a look,
It must be written somewhere, in
someone's little book.

Tranklements, tranklements! Has such
a delightful ring,
I'd really like to use it, but where?
That's the thing.

It tinkles so nicely when paired up
with trinkets,
It mysteriously conjures up thoughts
of secrets.

Trinkets and tranklements, just say it
to yourself.

It rolls beautifully around your
tongue, I just keep saying it to myself.

Trinkets and tranklements, well we all
know what they are,
We should use these words more
often, even in the car.

I bet your glove box is full of them, I
dare you to have a look!
But why is the word 'tranklements'
not recorded in any book?

Take a look in your kitchen drawer,
there's another source for these.
But searching through the dictionary
will bring you to your knees!

Trinkets and tranklements, I just love
the sound that they make,
So I've decided to use
them…often…whatever it may take.
Trinkets and tranklements, trinkets
and tranklements.

What Can We Get for Dad?

What can we get for Dad?
There must be something he's not yet
had.
He's got socks galore,
And ties that cascade to the floor.
What can we get for Dad?

A pair of slippers to replace the old,
To keep his feet warm in the winter's
cold.
But last years slippers are still quite
good,
Maybe we should just give him a
Christmas pud.
Oh what can we get for Dad?

Some bottles of beer would bring him
some cheer,
But then he'd just fall asleep I fear.
A jigsaw puzzle to occupy his mind,

But would he have patience with all
those pieces to find.
Oh what can we get for Dad?

A book to read, a good idea,
But his eyes are failing and he'd hold
it too near.
A tin of toffees was his favourite treat,
But with not many teeth they'd be
difficult to eat.
Oh what can we get for Dad?

A Betterware book dropped into the
hall,
Packed with ideas of gadgets for all!
They'll help with old age,
Something useful on every page
There must be something there for
Dad!

A blanket with sleeves!
A thingy for scooping up leaves.

A huge pair of slippers you can put
both feet in,
A long handled grabber so you don't
do your back in!
Are *any* of these suitable for Dad?

The answer I think, after very much
thought,
My nerves feeling ever so taught,
Is a nice family meal at the local pub,
Where Dad can enjoy his favourite
grub!
THAT'S what we'll get for Dad!

Printed in Great Britain
by Amazon